Author:
Jen Green graduated from the University
of Sussex, England, with a Ph.D. in English
Literature in 1982. She has worked as an
editor and manager in children's publishing
for 15 years and is now a full-time writer. She
has written many nonfiction books for
children.

Artist:
Mark Bergin studied at Eastbo[urne]
College of Art and has specialized [in]
historical reconstructions, aviation, [and]
maritime subjects since 1983. He liv[es in]
Bexhill-on-Sea, England, with his wife and
three children.

Series creator:
David Salariya was born in Dundee,
Scotland. He has illustrated a wide range of
books and has created and designed many
new series for publishers both in the UK and
overseas. In 1989 he established The Salariya
Book Company. He lives in Brighton with his
wife, the illustrator Shirley Willis, and their
son Jonathan.

Additional artists:
Dave Antram
David Stewart

Editors:
Karen Barker Smith
Stephanie Cole

This edition first published in 2014 by Book House

Distributed by Black Rabbit Books
P.O. Box 3263
Mankato
Minnesota MN 56002

SALARIYA

2014 The Salariya Book Company Ltd

[Pri]nted in the United States of America.
Printed on paper from sustainable forests.

Cataloging-in-Publication Data is available
from the Library of Congress

ISBN: 978-1-908973-85-6

GODS & GODDESSES

IN THE DAILY LIFE OF THE

VIKINGS

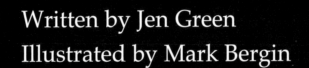

Written by Jen Green
Illustrated by Mark Bergin

BOOK HOUSE
a SALARIYA imprint

CONTENTS

INTRODUCTION

The Vikings were a bold, fierce, and sea-loving people from Scandinavia. From AD 793, the Vikings (also called Norsemen) launched a series of raids on ports throughout Europe. They would sail hundreds of miles and the first thing their victims were aware of was the appearance of warships on the horizon. Bands of Viking warriors rushed ashore, snatching up all the treasure they could carry before returning to the sea once again. Anyone who stood in their way was slaughtered. Such raids continued for the next 300 years.

They are best known for their bloodthirsty ways but the Vikings were also brave explorers, excellent craftsmen, great poets, and skilled traders. Most did not spend their lives on the high seas raiding and pillaging, but lived peacefully—fishing, farming, and tending their herds.

The Vikings believed that the universe was made up of Nine Worlds and that these were located on three levels. The uppermost level held the lands of the gods: Asgard, where the Aesir lived, and Vanaheim, home of the Vanir. The Aesir were warrior gods, and included Odin, Thor, and Tyr. The Vanir were peace-loving gods who looked after crops and fertility. The middle level of the Viking universe held Jotunheim, home of the giants, and Midgard (Earth), the land of humans. The lowest level included a fiery world called Muspell and icy Niflheim.

Many myths and stories were told about the gods' powers and deeds. For most of the Viking period, these stories were passed down the generations by word of mouth, but later some of the myths were recorded in writing. Such stories have told us much of what we know today about the Viking way of life.

ODIN
CHIEF OF THE GODS: VIKING SOCIETY

FAMILY

Wife Frigg
Brothers Ve, Vili
Sons Balder, Bragi,
  Heimdall, Hemrod,
  Hoder, Thor, Vali,
  Vidar

The Vikings came from what is now known as Scandinavia: Norway, Sweden, and Denmark. From the late 8th century, they began to raid coastal settlements in Europe and Russia. Later they established trading centers in some of these places. In the 9th century they settled in Iceland and from there explored lands farther west, including Greenland and Newfoundland in Canada.

Odin was the powerful chief of the Viking gods. He was known as the All-father because he created the earth, humans, and animals, but he was not a kindly god. Odin ruled Asgard, the realm of the gods, from his great hall, Valhalla. As god of battle he caused wars by throwing down his spear. Odin was cunning and clever. He gave one of his eyes in exchange for a drink from the Spring of Knowledge. Odin's many children included the gods Thor, Balder, Heimdall, and Bragi.

INSIDE STORY

Odin was one of the first Viking gods. From the beginning of time he and his brothers, Ve and Vili, were at war with another race of supernatural beings, the giants. The three brothers killed the giant Ymir and used his body to make Midgard—the Earth. Later, Odin created the first man and woman, Ask and Embla, from an ash and an elm-tree root.

This stone (below) is carved with runes, the letters of the Viking alphabet. These symbols were thought to be magical and to ward off danger. Odin learned the secret of runes in the land of the dead and later taught humans the script.

Map showing Viking raids and settlements around the 9th century

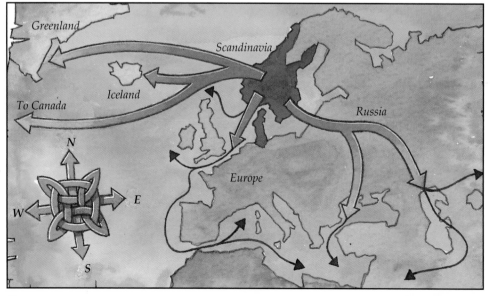

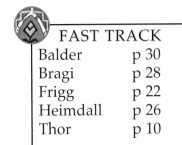

CHIEFS AND THEIR PEOPLE

Not all Vikings enjoyed equal status, and neither did their gods. Just as Odin was lord of Asgard, so each Viking community had its own lord or chief, who ruled from a great hall. At feasts the chief sat in a high chair, raised above the ordinary people. Viking society was divided into three classes: jarls (noblemen), karls (freemen), and thralls (slaves).

Women were the same class as their husbands. Noblemen were often wealthy landowners and many became local chieftains. Most Vikings were freemen, who worked as farmers, fishermen, traders, or craftsmen. Thralls had few rights and these people were bought and sold like cattle. Some had been captured in battle, others were the children of slaves.

FAST TRACK	
Balder	p 30
Bragi	p 28
Frigg	p 22
Heimdall	p 26
Thor	p 10

Chief

Classes of Viking society

Jarl

Karl

Thrall

THOR
GOD OF STORMS AND FARMING

This bronze figure of Thor (above) was found in Iceland and dates back to around AD 1000.

Thor, god of storms, was the most popular Viking god, especially among farmers. He was Odin's eldest son, but unlike his father, Thor was rather slow-witted and relied on brawn rather than brains. He was huge and amazingly strong, with fiery-red hair and a flaming temper to match. He did nothing by halves and loved eating, drinking, and fighting. Thor's favorite weapon was a mighty hammer, which he hurled like a thunderbolt. Lightning sparked from his chariot as he rode across the sky.

FAMILY
Father Odin
Mother Jorth
Wife Sif
Brothers Balder, Bragi, Heimdall, Hemrod, Hoder, Tyr
Sons Magni, Modi

FAST TRACK
Freya   p 24
Odin   p 8

INSIDE STORY

Thor was parted from his beloved hammer only once, when it was stolen by a giant named Thrym. Thrym declared he would only return the hammer if the goddess Freya became his wife. Thor agreed, but disguised himself as Freya for the wedding. At the ceremony, Thrym produced Thor's hammer and placed it on the "bride's" knee for her to swear by. Thor immediately sprang to his feet and slaughtered Thrym and all the wedding guests.

Thor's hammer, Mjollnir, was a magic weapon. It always hit its target and then flew straight back into his hand. It also protected Thor from harm. Vikings carried tiny "Thor" hammers as lucky charms or wore them as jewelry, like this pendant (right). At wedding feasts it was customary for the bride and groom to exchange their vows on Thor's hammer.

VIKING FARMS

Thor's influence over the weather made him vital to agriculture and he was married to Sif, a harvest goddess. Farmers prayed to both Thor and Sif for good harvests. The Vikings grew wheat, rye, oats, and barley to produce grain, which was then ground into flour using stones called querns. The flour was used to make porridge and bread. Viking farmers also kept animals. Horses helped with plowing; sheep, cows, and goats produced milk for making butter and cheese and provided meat and hides. Geese, pigs, and chickens were also reared for their meat. Many farms had their own smithy, where tools such as plows and sickles were made and repaired.

Farmhouse

Smithy

TYR
GOD OF JUSTICE AND SPORT

Tyr was strong, honorable, and courageous. He became god of law and order because he never broke his word. Frigg was Tyr's mother but the identity of his father is unclear: it was either Odin or, more likely, the frost giant, Hymir. Tyr was known as a brave god who lost his hand to a wolf-monster called Fenrir because of a promise the gods had made (see Inside Story, opposite).

Viking society was quite democratic for its time, with laws that applied to everyone, rich or poor. Even chieftains and great warriors like the one shown on this carving (above) had to obey the law.

FAMILY
Father Hymir or Odin
Mother Frigg
Brothers Balder, Bragi, Heimdall, Hemrod, Hoder, Thor

Tyr was also god of sport and athletes. Favorite Viking sports included wrestling (below), betting on stallions in horse fights, and swimming in summer. In the cold Scandinavian winters people skated and sledded.

The Vikings loved games, particularly if they involved gambling. On long winter nights, dice and a version of checkers were popular. By the 12th century the Vikings were playing chess. These chessmen (below), made of walrus tusk, were found on the Isle of Lewis in Scotland.

LAW AND ORDER

To outsiders the Vikings seemed to be a violent and lawless race. However, Viking society did have a code of law. Each community had a ruling council called a Thing, which decided local matters. All noblemen and freemen could be part of the Thing, but not women or slaves. These councils acted as courts and imposed penalties on wrongdoers. Midsummer Things lasted a week or more. People came from far and wide to camp, meet friends, and enjoy sports such as wrestling and horse fighting. In Iceland, a national council called the Althing made decisions affecting the whole country. In effect, it was an early form of parliament.

INSIDE STORY

The fierce wolf-monster Fenrir was the son of the god Loki and the giantess Angrboda. He was so wild that the gods decided to contain him. Claiming they wanted to test his strength, they put him in chains, but Fenrir broke them easily. Next, the gods had an unbreakable magic chain made. Fenrir was suspicious and only agreed to be chained again if one of the gods placed a hand in his mouth as a mark of faith. Only Tyr was brave enough to do it. Fenrir bit his hand off as he struggled to break free, but the chain held fast.

AEGIR
GOD OF THE SEA: SHIPS AND FISHING

Gods of the sea were very important to the Vikings as a seafaring people. As expert sailors they used the oceans for fishing, trading, and to travel around Scandinavia. They also sailed to distant lands such as Iceland and Greenland and set up colonies there. Viking fishermen used nets or rods with winders to catch cod and herring. In the icy northern waters, they used harpoons to catch seals, walruses, and whales.

This scene (below) from the Bayeux Tapestry in Normandy, France, shows Viking ship-building skills. Viking craft were very advanced for their day. A shallow keel running along the bottom made the ships stable and speedy. Helmsmen steered using an oar lashed to the side, near the stern (rear). Warships carried a large, square sail and were rowed by up to fifty men.

Aegir and his wife, Ran, ruled over the oceans. Their home was a hall on the seabed that gleamed with treasure from shipwrecks. Sometimes they were kind toward humans, sending calm seas and driving shoals of fish into fishermen's nets. However, sometimes they would raise tempests with howling winds and crashing waves to capsize ships. Aegir and Ran would then swim upward with a giant net made by Loki and drag sailors to their doom. The drowned men were treated to mead and feasts in Aegir's hall.

FAST TRACK
Loki	p 18
Thor	p 10
Tyr	p 12

FAMILY
Wife Ran
Children Nine daughters (the Wave Maidens)

Sternpost

Planks made by splitting logs

INSIDE STORY

Sweet, strong mead was the gods' favorite drink but once the gods of Asgard ran out of it. Thor and Tyr went down to Aegir's hall to ask him to brew some more. Aegir agreed but said he would need a giant cauldron for brewing. Tyr remembered that the giant Hymir had such a cauldron. After many adventures, Thor succeeded in winning the cauldron, which he delivered to Aegir. After that, Aegir always brewed the gods' mead.

Some Viking ships had weather vanes like this (right) which showed which way the wind was blowing. Sailors kept a close eye on currents, winds, and waves. In coastal waters they navigated using familiar landmarks. Far out to sea, they used the sun and stars to work out where they were.

SHIPBUILDING

The Vikings built two main types of boats: warships called longships and cargo boats called knorrs. Longships were slim and fast. They were light and easy to maneuver in shallow water, which made them good for raiding. Knorrs were shorter, wider, and sturdy. They could be used to transport animals, passengers, and heavy loads.

High prow

Hull made from overlapping planks

NJORD
GOD OF COASTS, SEA WINDS, AND TRADERS

Foreign items found in Scandinavia, such as this Indian statue of Buddha, show that the Vikings traded with distant countries. Merchants sailed north to obtain furs and walrus ivory and south for sweet wine, fine swords, and glassware. Silk and spices from the east were always in demand.

FAMILY
Wife Skadi
Son Frey
Daughter Freya

Njord was a handsome, kind god who often helped human sailors. As patron of traders, he raised favorable winds that helped merchants' ships and calmed storms before they struck the coast. Njord's hall lay on the seashore. His wife, Skadi, was goddess of hunting. She loved the mountains and hated the ocean. Njord couldn't bear to leave the sea for long, so the couple didn't get on very well.

INSIDE STORY
Njord met Skadi when the goddess of hunting visited Asgard. She came in search of vengeance because the gods had killed her father, a giant called Thiazi. To soothe her, the gods said she could marry one of them, but she had to choose by looking only at their feet. They all hid behind a screen. Skadi chose a pair of shapely feet she hoped belonged to a handsome god called Balder, but they were Njord's, so she had to marry him instead.

Swedish Vikings sailed southeast down the rivers of Russia to reach the city of Kiev and the Black and Caspian seas. Kiev lay on an ancient trading route that led to the east. There, Viking merchants traded furs, iron, honey, wax, and slaves for Arab silver, eastern spices, and Chinese silk. Eventually, some Vikings settled permanently in Kiev.

TRADING PORTS

Scandinavia was a wild, mountainous, and often snowy land with few decent roads for travelers. Most goods arrived by sea. Viking settlements grew up along rivers or on rugged coasts that offered sheltered harbors for shipping. Here you can see a cargo of German wine being unloaded from a merchant's ship that has just arrived at the quay (above).

LOKI

GOD OF MISCHIEF AND TRICKERY: VIKING RAIDS

FAMILY
First wife Angrboda
Second wife Sigyn
Children Hel, Fenrir,
Jormungand,
Sleipnir

This stone (above) commemorated the first-ever Viking raid in AD 793. A band of warriors attacked the Christian monastery at Lindisfarne in northeast England and made off with a rich haul of loot.

Handsome and witty, Loki was a god of many talents. His jokes and tricks made the other gods roar with laughter. He was also a skillful shape-shifter who could transform himself into a fly, a horse, a fish, or a bird. In the early days, Loki was a harmless prankster, but later he turned bitter and spiteful and made trouble for the gods. The Vikings were fascinated by Loki, perhaps because some of them were also troublemakers, earning a living through raiding.

IN SEARCH OF LOOT

The raid on Lindisfarne was soon followed by further attacks on ports in England, Ireland, and Scotland. By the mid-800s, Vikings were raiding distant targets in France, Italy, and Spain. Villages yielded hauls of weapons, tools, slaves, and livestock. Monasteries held treasures such as gold and silver cups and jeweled books and boxes. Monasteries were popular targets because the peace-loving monks could not defend themselves.

FAST TRACK

This gilt mount from a horse's bridle (left) was part of the horse trappings of a Viking raider. It was found in Lincolnshire, England, where a lot of raids took place during the 9th and 10th centuries.

Viking raiders coming ashore

INSIDE STORY

Loki had several wives, including the giantess Angrboda, but he was not faithful to her. Once Loki turned himself into a mare and cantered off with a giant's horse. Later he returned with an eight-legged foal, Sleipnir, whom he had mothered. He gave the magical horse to Odin as a gift.

Viking raiders were ruthless warriors who thought that death in battle was honorable. They believed that if they died fighting, they would be taken to Valhalla, where Odin himself would welcome them. They would live in the land of the gods forever, fighting all day and feasting all night.

Viking warships each had a tall prow carved in the shape of a dragon or sea monster (right). These tall ships inspired terror when they appeared on the horizon, looking like black birds of prey. All over Europe, villagers huddling around their fires, and monks in their cold cells, trembled in fear of the Vikings. "O lord, deliver us from the fury of the Norsemen" became a common prayer.

FREY
GOD OF FERTILITY: CHILDREN

As god of fertility, Frey blessed marriages with children. Frey figurines like the bronze one above may have been given to couples at their wedding as lucky charms. Farmers also prayed to Frey in spring, to grant a rich harvest later in the year.

Frey was one of the Vanir, the gods of peace and prosperity. He had come to live in Asgard with his father Njord and his twin sister, Freya. Frey rode a chariot pulled by a golden boar. He had a magic ship called Skidbladnir, which was large enough to transport all the gods, their chariots, and horses, yet could also be small enough to fit inside a pocket. Frey's wife was Gerd, a beautiful frost giantess and goddess of the Northern Lights. Couples prayed to Frey to give them strong, healthy children.

FAMILY
Father Njord
Sister Freya
Wife Gerd
Son Fiolnir

Viking children had to help at home from an early age.

Some Viking children had toy ships, dolls, horses, and games to play with. These miniature figures (left) are called "hnefi" and belonged to a game called "hnefatafl," a bit like today's checkers. In summer, when not doing chores, children went swimming and played bat and ball games. In winter, they went sledding and skating and had snowball fights.

VIKING CHILDREN

Viking children had to obey their parents, but were encouraged to show plenty of spirit. The Vikings didn't have schools, so children learned all the skills they needed from their parents and other grown-ups at home.

Cooking a meal over a stone hearth

Viking children had to grow up quickly. From a young age, they were expected to do their share of household chores. In spring they collected birds' eggs; in the fall they picked berries and mushrooms. Girls learned cooking, spinning, and weaving. Boys fetched firewood and helped look after the farm animals. They also learned fighting skills and practiced with toy swords, spears, and shields. Boys as young as 16 were taken on raids.

INSIDE STORY

Frey fell in love with Gerd after spotting her from Asgard, but she lived in Jotunheim, the land of the giants. The gods were not allowed there, so Frey sent his father's servant, Skirnir, to woo her for him. Skirnir tried flattery, then bribery, but Gerd wasn't interested. In the end, he threatened her with a terrible curse. She finally met Frey, softened, and married him. Later they had a son named Fiolnir.

FRIGG
GODDESS OF WOMEN: MARRIAGE AND HOME LIFE

This little silver and gilt figure may represent Frigg or a wealthy woman in her best clothes. She is wearing a shawl, a flowing underdress, and rich jewelry, including a row of beads and a large ring brooch.

The goddess Frigg was Odin's wife and queen of Asgard. Of all the gods, she alone was allowed to share Odin's throne. Frigg shared her husband's power to see into the future, but she never told what she saw. She was the mother of several gods including Balder, Bragi, Tyr, and Hemrod. She defended her children passionately if anyone criticized them. Viking women, especially mothers, looked to her for protection. Frigg was generally faithful to Odin, but sometimes outwitted her husband to get her own way.

INSIDE STORY
Frigg and Odin both took a great interest in humans. Once, during a war between the Vandal tribe and the Winiler tribe, the gods found themselves on opposite sides: Odin supported the Vandals, and Frigg the Winilers. On the eve of battle, Odin declared that the army he saw first in the morning would be victorious. His couch faced the Vandals' camp. When he was asleep, Frigg turned the couch around, so Odin saw the Winilers first and had to give them victory.

FAMILY
Husband Odin
Sons Balder, Bragi, Hemrod, Hoder, Tyr

As well as sewing, weaving, and spinning, women's duties included cooking, cleaning, looking after the children and animals, and making medicines. Wealthy women had slaves to do heavy work. Keys symbolized a woman's responsibilities. Wives were usually in charge of lockable storerooms and the casket where family jewelry and other valuables were kept. The wife took over the running of the family farm or business if her husband was away and would take the lead in defending her home if it was attacked.

FAST TRACK
Balder	p 30
Bragi	p 28
Hemrod	p 34
Odin	p 8
Tyr	p 12

Weaving on a loom

Spinning wool

Women and men were not equal in Viking society. A wealthy man might have several wives, who were all expected to be faithful to him. However, Viking women had more rights than many women of their day. They could own land and property, and could get a divorce if they were badly treated.

FAMILY
Father Njord
Brother Frey
Husband Od

FAST TRACK

Freya, the Viking goddess of love, was Frey's twin sister. She had once been married to a god called Od, but he disappeared and deserted her. Freya wept golden tears but she then consoled herself by taking a series of lovers, both humans and gods. Freya was very beautiful and had a weakness for all beautiful things, particularly jewelry. This weakness led Odin to bribe her into becoming a god of war (see Inside Story, below).

Some valuable rings and brooches have been found in hoards of buried Viking treasure. This silver and gold brooch was discovered in a Viking grave in Sweden.

Like Freya, the Vikings were very fond of jewelry. Items such as this brooch (above) with enamel-work and precious stones were works of art.

INSIDE STORY

Freya was the proud owner of a beautiful necklace called Brisingamen. It had been made by four dwarfs, the Brisings, who were master-craftsmen. Freya had to do favors for all four to get the necklace. When Odin heard about it, he was angry. He ordered Loki to steal the necklace, then told Freya she could have it back only if she agreed to become goddess of battle. Freya wanted the necklace so badly that she agreed. From then on, half of all warriors killed in battle went to live in her hall and the other half went to join Odin in Valhalla.

Ring-and-pin brooch

Box brooch, which contains tiny tweezers

Animal-shaped brooch

Buckle

Silver toiletry articles

VIKING JEWELRY

Both men and women wore jewelry as decoration and to fasten their clothing. Men fastened their cloaks with ring-and-pin brooches on the right shoulder, which meant their right arm was free to grab their sword. They also wore heavy neck rings called torques. The finest jewelry was made of gold and silver. Less well-off people wore bronze, copper, or pewter items. Even poor people had simple brooches made of bone.

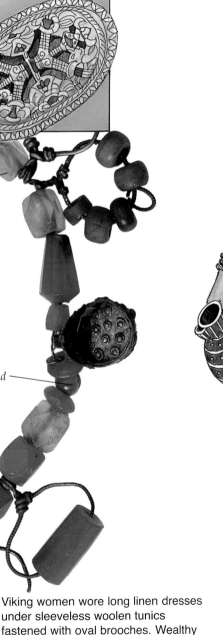

Glass bead

This beautiful necklace of glass, amber, and cornelian beads is hung with silver trinkets. The Vikings did not make their own glass, but imported it from countries farther south. Silver coins and trinkets came from the east.

Amber bead

Cornelian bead

Viking women wore long linen dresses under sleeveless woolen tunics fastened with oval brooches. Wealthy women had embroidered tunics. In cold weather, a cloak or shawl over the shoulders was pinned with another brooch (right).

A prosperous married Viking woman wore fine jewelry and decorated woven outer garments.

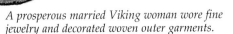

HEIMDALL

WATCHMAN OF THE GODS: VIKING DEFENSES

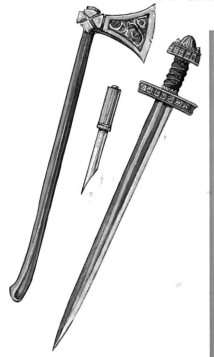

Axes and swords were the weapons of Viking watchmen and other soldiers. They also carried spears and wooden shields.

Heimdall was a tall, handsome, intelligent god possessed of amazing senses. He could hear the sound of wool growing on a sheep's back and see a great distance both night and day. For this reason he became watchman of the gods. Heimdall guarded Bifrost, the rainbow bridge that stretched down from Asgard to Midgard (Earth). His father was Odin and his mothers were said to be the nine Wave Maidens, the daughters of Aegir, who all gave birth to him at once.

Viking warriors wore metal helmets to protect their heads. Some, like the one pictured left, had a ridge on top, a nose-guard, and "goggles" to protect the eyes. Viking helmets are often imagined as having horns on the top, but no such armor has ever been found.

INSIDE STORY

On a trip to Earth, Heimdall founded the three classes that made up Viking society. He visited a lord's hall, a farm, and a peasant hovel in turn. An old couple from each fed and welcomed him. Nine months later, all three women gave birth. The poorest woman bore a hardworking son called Thrall, the ancestor of all peasants. The farmer's wife bore a strong son called Karl, from whom all farmers were descended. The noblewoman's clever, warlike son, Jarl, founded the Viking ruling class.

FAST TRACK

Aegir   p 14
Odin   p 8

FAMILY

Father Odin
Mothers The nine Wave Maidens
Brothers Balder, Bragi, Hemrod, Hoder, Thor, Tyr

TOWN DEFENSES

Viking towns had defenses to protect them from neighboring tribes and even foreign armies seeking revenge for raids on their countries. High ramparts of earth supported a protected walkway from which sentries could look out over the surrounding land. Gates in the ramparts allowed travelers to leave and enter the town. By day, the gates stood open, but they were closed and barred at night.

BRAGI

GOD OF POETRY AND KNOWLEDGE: ENTERTAINMENT

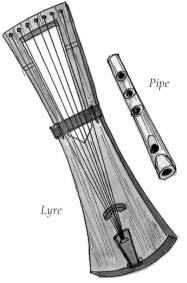

Pipe

Lyre

Viking skalds entertained their lords with long poems about the exploits of gods and human heroes. They played a stringed instrument called a lyre (above), and pipes made of deer or sheep bone were also used to make music.

Bragi's mother was either Frigg or a giantess called Gunnlod, whose father possessed a magical drink, the mead of poetry. Bragi was very clever and also a talented musician. Odin made him the skald, or court poet, of Asgard. His role was to entertain the gods at feasts with poetry and songs and to welcome dead heroes to Valhalla. Bragi's wife, Idunn, guarded the golden apples of immortality. These miraculous fruits kept the gods youthful and strong.

FAMILY
Father Odin
Mother Frigg or Gunnlod
Brothers Balder, Heimdall, Hemrod, Hoder, Thor, Tyr
Wife Idunn

Bragi inspired humans to write poetry and protected skalds, who were professional poets. Skalds held an important place in Viking society. Some were hired by lords to entertain their guests at feasts. They accompanied their masters to war so they could recite verses to bring victory. Other skalds moved from village to village telling stories. In this way, Viking myths were passed on by word of mouth and from one generation to the next.

As god of knowledge, Bragi encouraged humans to use runes, the Viking form of writing. The runic alphabet had only 16 letters. All were formed of straight lines, which made them easy to carve on picture stones like this one (below) or on bone or wood.

Skald

INSIDE STORY

Bragi's wife, Idunn, was kidnapped by the giant Thiazi after Loki had tricked her into leaving Asgard. Without Idunn's apples, the gods started to grow old. They threatened to kill Loki unless he got the apples back. Loki turned himself into a falcon and entered Thiazi's hall, then changed Idunn into a nut and carried her off with the apples. Thiazi turned himself into an eagle and chased Loki, but the gods singed his wings with fire and he crashed to the ground.

A skald entertains his lord and guests at a feast (below). Wealthy chiefs gave feasts to celebrate births, weddings, harvests, and successful raids. A great feast might last as long as two weeks. Yule was a major feast which happened around January 12, to mark the passing of winter. At feasts, the ale, mead, and wine flowed freely and everyone ate and drank as much as possible. Some wise lords posted sentries outside to raise the alarm if an enemy attacked while most people were drunk.

FAST TRACK

Frigg	p 22
Loki	p 18
Odin	p 8

Chief

Skald

BALDER
GOD OF LIGHT AND HAPPINESS: FUNERALS

Balder, son of Odin and Frigg, was gentle, wise, and just. Everyone loved him—everyone except Loki. The god of mischief was jealous of Balder and schemed against him. Balder began to have nightmares and a seer foretold he would soon die a horrible death. Frigg was frantic with worry. She made everything swear it would not hurt Balder. Fire, water, weapons, dangerous animals, and even illnesses swore. Mistletoe was the only thing that Frigg did not ask to swear because it seemed such a harmless plant.

FAMILY

Father Odin
Mother Frigg
Brothers Bragi, Heimdall, Hemrod, Hoder, Thor, Tyr
Wife Nanna
Son Forseti

Overwhelmed with sorrow at Balder's death, the gods gave him a hero's funeral. They pulled his ship to shore, placed him inside, and piled it with treasure. Balder's wife Nanna was so grief-stricken that she died of a broken heart, so she was put in too. Then the gods set fire to the boat and a friendly giantess called Hyrrokin pushed it out to sea.

Viking ship funeral

SHIP FUNERALS AND BURIAL

The Vikings believed in life after death. Noblemen and noblewomen were buried in ships that would ferry them to the next world. Less wealthy people were buried in graves marked by stones arranged in the shape of a ship. This Viking burial site (below) is in Sweden.

Wooden post carved in the shape of a dragon's head and decorated with delicate swirling patterns.

In 1903, the remains of a Viking ship burial were discovered at Oseberg in Norway. The bodies of a wealthy woman and her servant had been placed in a boat and buried in wet clay, which had preserved the remains. Treasures including a carved wagon and three sleds, fine furniture, tapestries, and five mysterious dragon posts like this one (above) had been placed in the grave. The carved wooden posts were attached to long planks. They probably had religious meaning, but no one can be sure.

Some Viking kings and wealthy nobles were given a ship burial like Balder when they died. Their bodies were dressed in fine clothes and placed in a boat with treasure. Animals and even servants might be killed so they could accompany their chief to the afterlife. Then the boat was either burned or buried beneath a huge mound of earth. In AD 922 an Arab traveler named Ibn Fadlan witnessed a Viking ship burial in Russia. The dead man was placed in a tent on the boat. Two horses, two cows, a dog, and a slave girl were sacrificed to serve him in the next world. An old woman known as the Angel of Death removed the knife that had been used to make the sacrifices. Then logs were stacked up around the ship to make a funeral pyre and the whole thing was set alight.

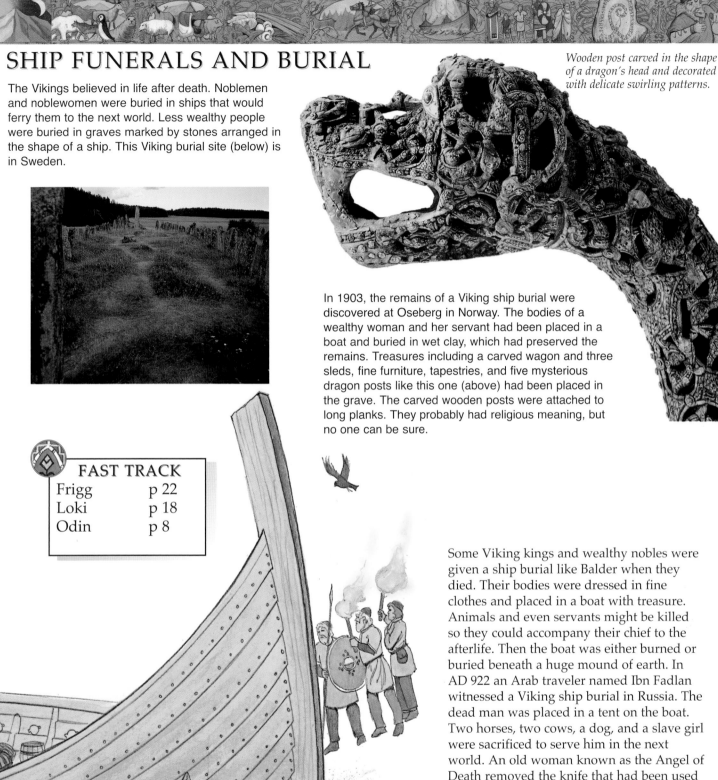

Angel of Death

HEL
GODDESS OF THE DEAD: DEATH

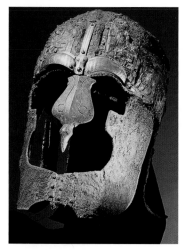

This warrior's iron and bronze helmet was found in a Viking grave in Sweden. Vikings were often buried with treasured possessions that might help them in the afterlife. These objects are known as grave goods. Men were given tools or weapons; women might have cooking pots or needles. The graves of wealthy people often held gold and silver. Even peasants were buried with a favorite tool.

Hel, goddess of the dead, presided over a cold, misty kingdom in the Viking underworld, which was known as Niflheim. She ruled over all dead people except brave warriors who had died in battle, who went to live with Odin or Freya in Asgard. Hel was the daughter of Loki and the giantess Angrboda and was monstrous. Above the waist, she looked like a beautiful woman, but below the waist her body was a rotting corpse. After their deaths, Balder and his wife Nanna went to live with Hel.

FAMILY
Father Loki
Mother Angrboda
Brothers Fenrir, Jormungand

Swords would be needed by warriors fighting for Odin in the afterlife. These and other weapons were often placed in soldiers' graves, like this sword found in Denmark.

INSIDE STORY

Frigg was overcome with grief after Balder's death and couldn't accept that her son had died. Then she had an idea. Maybe Hel would be prepared to release Balder from the underworld if one of the gods went to plead with her. Everyone hesitated because the journey to Niflheim was so long and dangerous. Eventually Hemrod, Balder's brother, said he would travel to the underworld.

Silver coins placed in a grave might also have been useful in the afterlife. These (above) show Viking longships.

GRAVE BURIAL

Only kings and rich chieftains were given ship burials. Other people were mostly buried in graves lined with wood, which might then be covered with a mound of earth. Townsfolk were buried in cemeteries outside the city walls.

Farmers were often buried near their home in the countryside. Burial customs varied throughout Scandinavia and some people were cremated, but most, like this warrior (below), were buried with grave goods.

Grave goods included the warrior's weapons, drinking vessels, and stirrups so he could ride in the afterlife.

The warrior's favorite horses were slaughtered to be buried with him.

Relatives grieve while comrades toss gifts of money into the grave.

HEMROD
MESSENGER OF THE GODS: TRAVEL AND TRAVELERS

A Viking horseman crosses a river at a ford, where the water is shallow. Such crossing points were often marked by tall standing stones.

Hemrod was god of travel and patron of travelers. Vikings setting out on long journeys prayed to him for luck. Hemrod helped Bragi welcome warriors to Valhalla and ran errands for the gods. He volunteered to visit Hel to plead for Balder's life and descended for nine days and nights until he reached Niflheim. Hemrod told Hel that everyone and everything in the Nine Worlds wept for Balder and begged her to release him. Hel agreed to let Balder go if everyone was truly weeping, but said she would keep him if not.

INSIDE STORY
Hemrod returned to Asgard to tell Odin and Frigg what Hel had promised about Balder. They set off through the Nine Worlds, persuading everyone and everything to weep for their son. Gods, humans, animals, even stones and trees began to weep for Balder. So did many of the giants, but one old giantess refused to weep for him. The bargain with Hel was broken and Balder remained in Niflheim. The old giantess was actually Loki in disguise.

Hole for reins

This picture (above) shows half of a curved harness that would have rested on a horse's back. The reins passed through the hole in the center. Such harnesses transferred the weight of the cart to the horse's back to make pulling easier. This richly decorated harness was probably only used at ceremonies and special occasions.

Goods traveling by land were carried in carts pulled by horses (below) or oxen. Some carts had detachable bodies that could be lifted off the wheels and loaded into boats. In winter, heavy loads were transported in sleighs pulled by horses or reindeer. Horseshoes with spikes helped horses to keep their footing on the ice.

TRAVELING BY LAND

Scandinavia is a rugged land where lakes, bogs, and mountains made land travel difficult. Viking travelers faced many hazards, including deep mud, bad weather, and bandits. Along key routes, roads were sometimes paved with wood. Road builders laid flat planks over a wooden framework and sprinkled sand on top to make the surface less slippery. The work was organized by the local chief and paid for by taxes. In winter, snow covered the land and streams froze over, which made travel easier. People used skis, skates, and snowshoes to get around.

This brooch (above) shows a mounted warrior armed with a long sword. Like the god Hemrod, many Vikings were expert riders. The sons of noblemen often learned to ride horses as soon as they could walk.

A layer of sand on top made the road less slippery in wet weather.

Long, flat planks were made by splitting logs with metal chisels.

Workers laid planks end to end or crossways.

SIGURD

HERO AND SWORDSMAN: BLACKSMITHS AND CRAFTS

INSIDE STORY

Sigurd went on to rescue a goddess called Brynhild, one of Odin's warrior-maidens, from a castle where she had fallen into a charmed sleep. Brynhild fell in love with Sigurd, but he spurned her and married another woman, Gudrun. Brynhild arranged to have Sigurd murdered, but at his funeral she was so overcome with sorrow that she threw herself onto the funeral pyre.

Sigurd was not a god, but was a bold and courageous human who became a hero. His father died so he was brought up by his uncle, the blacksmith Regin. Regin knew of a treasure hoard that was guarded by the dragon Fafnir. When Sigurd was old enough, Regin forged him a mighty sword and he killed Fafnir. Sigurd roasted the dragon's heart and tasted his blood, which gave him the power to understand birdsong. The birds told Sigurd that Regin was planning to kill him, so he killed the smith and took the gold.

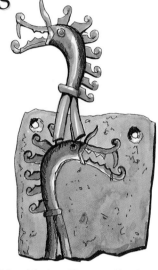

Viking blacksmiths practiced a range of different metalworking crafts, including welding and casting. Ornaments such as this curly-maned dragon (above) were made by pouring hot, molten metal into a mold. This mold was made by carving the design into soapstone.

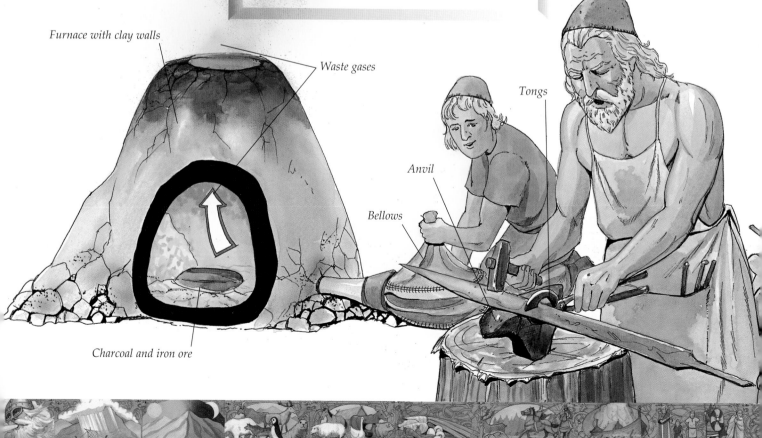

Furnace with clay walls

Waste gases

Tongs

Anvil

Bellows

Charcoal and iron ore

This fine axhead (above) is decorated with inlaid silver foil to form a swirling pattern. The smith first cut grooves into the blade using a hard, sharp chisel, then hammered silver wire into the grooves.

These wooden panels (above and below) are from a church in Norway and illustrate the story of Sigurd and Regin. In the top panel, Sigurd tests a poor-quality sword by breaking it on Regin's anvil. In the lower panel, Regin forges a sword from a broken blade, which had belonged to Sigurd's father, Sigmund. A helper works the bellows at the forge.

SMITHS AT WORK

At the blacksmith's forge, iron was made by heating iron ore with charcoal inside a very hot furnace. An assistant worked the bellows to fan the flames. The blacksmith then shaped the iron by hammering it on his anvil. As well as swords, axes, and other weapons, blacksmiths made tools such as chisels, cooking pots, and locks and keys.

THE NORNS

WEAVERS OF FATE: WEAVING

Spinning and weaving were vital crafts in Viking society. In every household, women wove woollen threads into cloth to make tunics, cloaks, and other garments for the whole family. Bedding and tapestries were also woven. Clay and stone weights such as these (above) were used in the weaving process, to hold the threads taut on the loom.

The Norns were three old sisters: Skuld (Being), Urd (Fate), and Verdandi (Necessity). They could see into the past, present, and future and the fate of everyone, even the gods, lay in their hands. The Norns wove huge, intricate tapestries of colored threads and each thread represented a life. The Norns lived by a well in Asgard, where they tended a sacred tree called Yggdrasil. They repeatedly warned that Loki would bring disaster to Asgard, but no one took any notice, until Loki misbehaved at a great feast.

INSIDE STORY

After Balder's death, Loki avoided the other gods, who had become deeply suspicious of him. They continued to mourn Balder, until Aegir decided to throw a banquet to end the mourning. Loki was not invited to the feast, but he turned up anyway. He proceeded to recite a long, rude poem which insulted each of the gods in turn and gave away all their secrets. When Thor threatened him with his hammer, Loki fled. The gods decided to punish Loki, but they had to catch him first.

Viking women used a variety of tools when weaving. Shears for cutting (a), a reel for winding thread (b), a spindle for spinning thread (c), a comb for smoothing wool (d), and a loom weight (e) are shown below.

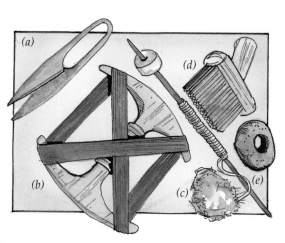

Rich tapestries hung on the walls of wealthy Viking houses, providing warmth and color. This twelfth-century tapestry (right) from the church of Skog in Sweden is thought to show three of the Viking gods: Odin, Thor, and Frey. One-eyed Odin is on the left, Thor is in the middle with his hammer. Frey in a red robe is on the right.

SPINNING AND WEAVING

An upright loom stood by the wall in most Viking households. Rows of upright threads, called the warp, hung from a beam at the top and were pulled taut by weights. Horizontal threads, called the weft, were woven in to make the cloth. Viking women were also expert at spinning, dyeing, and embroidery. Here one woman uses the loom while another stitches a tapestry and a third weaves a belt.

Loom

Woven belt

Stitching a tapestry

Weights

PRAYING

TO THE GODS: VIKING WORSHIP

In Viking towns such as Uppsala in Sweden, the Vikings worshipped in temples which held large statues of Odin, Thor, and other gods. Rituals also took place outdoors, in holy places such as groves of trees, springs, and rocky outcrops. To win the gods' favor, people offered gifts of jewelry, tools, and weapons. They also sacrificed animals and sometimes even humans—most probably slaves. Viking lords and chiefs led their people in religious ceremonies celebrating special days such as harvest and Yule.

This beautiful carving (below) from the Viking church at Urnes in Scandinavia shows a deer eating the leaves of the world tree, Yggdrasil. This sacred tree had roots in each of the three levels that made up the Viking universe.

Several Viking gods were thought to have the power to see into the future. They included Odin (above), who had given one of his eyes to drink from the Spring of Knowledge, his wife Frigg, the Norns, and the goddess Freya. Priestesses of Freya toured Viking lands, leading ceremonies which allowed them to see the future. The head priestess would fall into a trance in which her spirit was believed to leave her body. When she awoke, she told local people what the future had in store.

This Viking lucky charm (above) combines the symbols of two religions, the Christian cross and Thor's hammer.

Christian missionaries began to spread their faith in Scandinavia and from the 10th to 11th century many Vikings worshipped both Christ and the Norse gods. Thor was the most popular Viking god, but more stories were told about Loki than any other deity. This was probably because Loki's mischief-making helped to explain the existence of "bad" things in the world, such as sickness, violence, and death.

This ornate object (left) is the top of a bishop's crozier— the staff that signified his status— found in Sweden. By the 9th century, the Vikings were surrounded by lands that had converted to Christianity. Merchants came into contact with Christians on trading journeys. They allowed Christians to bless them so they could do business with them. This new religion was also spread by slaves captured on Viking raids.

INSIDE STORY

After Aegir's banquet to end the mourning for Balder, Loki fled and went into hiding. He turned himself into a salmon and leaped into a stream, but the gods recognized him and caught him in a net. They imprisoned him in an underground cave and bound him tightly. Njord's wife, Skadi, placed a poisonous snake on the roof of the cave above him, so the venom dripped down onto his face. Loki's faithful wife, Sigyn, stood at his side and held a bowl to catch the poison.

Several foreign travelers who visited Viking settlements described how the Vikings worshipped. An Arab merchant reported seeing Viking traders in Russia bowing down in prayer before statues of their gods. In 1070 a German monk, Adam of Bremen, witnessed a nine-day religious festival at Uppsala. On each of the nine days, a man and various kinds of animals were sacrificed. Their bodies were hung on trees in a sacred grove. In the 10th century, another Arab traveler, visiting Denmark, reported that townspeople placed animal sacrifices on wooden scaffolding outside their houses to please the gods.

RAGNAROK

DOOM OF THE GODS

The myth of Ragnarok, like other Viking legends, was passed on by word of mouth for most of the Viking era. In the 13th century, several versions of the Viking myths were written down in long stories called sagas, which have survived to the present day.

Ragnarok will begin as the god Heimdall sounds his horn. The wolf-monster Fenrir will devour Odin, as shown in this 10th-century stone carving (below). Then Odin's son, Vidar, will kill Fenrir. Many of the gods and their enemies will die. The fire giant Surt will kill Frey and set Asgard on fire. Loki and Heimdall will slay one another. Thor will kill the serpent Jormungand, but will die from his poison. This is how the Vikings believed the forces of good and evil would be canceled out. The Earth would sink into the sea and almost all life would be wiped out.

The Vikings believed that sometime in the future, most of their gods would die in a great battle and the world would end. They called it Ragnarok, which means "doom of the gods." Ragnarok would be triggered by Balder's death and Loki's punishment. The conflict between the gods and the giants would become more violent and wars would break out among humans. A giant wolf would devour the sun and plunge the Earth into darkness. Most humans would die, but one couple would climb into the branches of the world tree, Yggdrasil. Then Loki and Fenrir would break free of their chains, and lead an army of giants against the gods.

This silver crucifix from Sweden indicates the gradual spread of Christianity through Viking lands. The process began in the early 800s and took more than two centuries.

Norwegian stave church

This Norwegian church (right), built around 1150, carries Christian crosses, as well as dragons' heads symbolizing the Viking religion. In 965, the Danish king Harald Bluetooth became a Christian. In 1024, King Olaf Haraldsson of Norway converted too. The people of both Denmark and Norway gradually followed their rulers' lead. Swedish Vikings held out against Christianity for many years, but by the late 11th century, they too had been converted. The removal of the old religion marked the end of the Viking age.

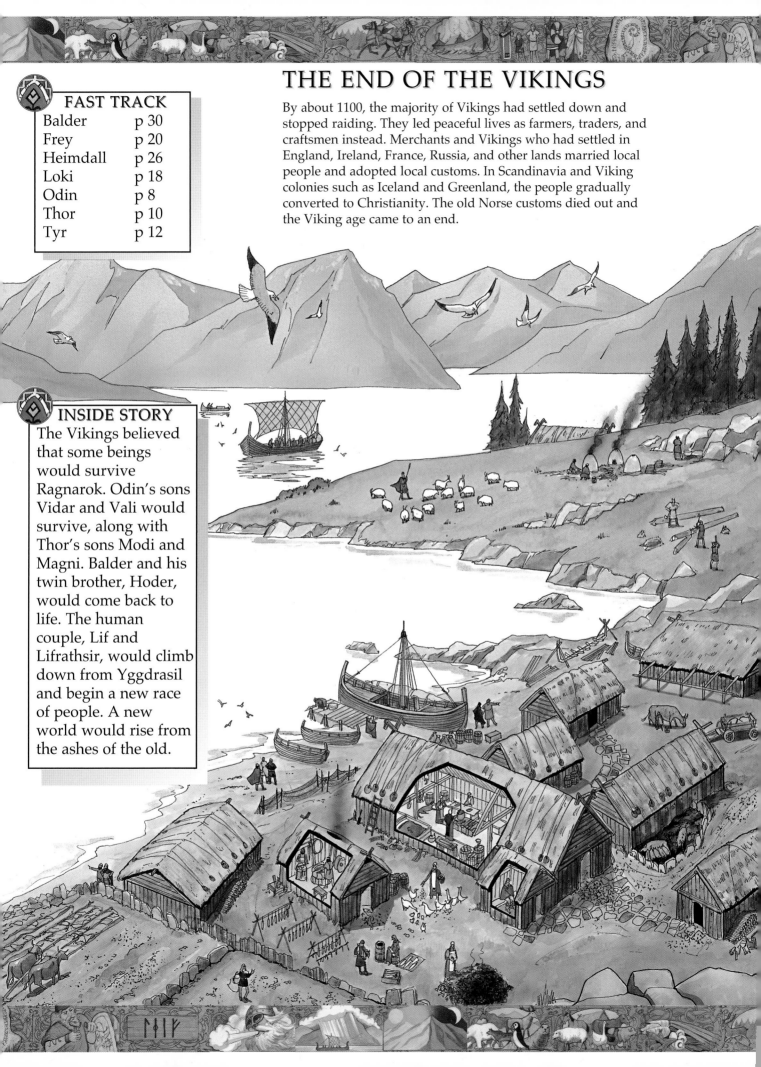

THE END OF THE VIKINGS

By about 1100, the majority of Vikings had settled down and stopped raiding. They led peaceful lives as farmers, traders, and craftsmen instead. Merchants and Vikings who had settled in England, Ireland, France, Russia, and other lands married local people and adopted local customs. In Scandinavia and Viking colonies such as Iceland and Greenland, the people gradually converted to Christianity. The old Norse customs died out and the Viking age came to an end.

INSIDE STORY

The Vikings believed that some beings would survive Ragnarok. Odin's sons Vidar and Vali would survive, along with Thor's sons Modi and Magni. Balder and his twin brother, Hoder, would come back to life. The human couple, Lif and Lifrathsir, would climb down from Yggdrasil and begin a new race of people. A new world would rise from the ashes of the old.

GLOSSARY

Althing The name of the national council that ruled Iceland during the Viking era.

Colony A settlement set up by people from another land.

Cornelian A red mineral often used as a gemstone.

Hull The body of a boat, the part that floats in the water.

Jarl A Viking nobleman. Many jarls were wealthy landowners.

Karl A freeman in Viking society. Many karls were farmers, fishermen, traders, or craftsmen.

Keel The long timber running along the underside of a boat.

Knorr A wide-bottomed, sturdy Viking boat used to ferry cargo, passengers, and animals.

Longship A long, fast, and narrow Viking warship.

Loom A machine used to weave cloth.

Mare A female horse.

Mead An alcoholic drink made of honey and spices.

Midgard The name for Earth in Viking mythology.

Missionary A person who travels overseas to spread their faith.

Norsemen Another name for Vikings.

Northern Lights Another name for aurora borealis, the streamers of light sometimes seen in the sky around the North Pole.

Prow The front of a ship.

Quern A hand-operated machine for crushing grain, made of two heavy stones. Grain is placed between the stones and is then crushed to make flour.

Rampart A high mound of earth topped by a wall, used for defense.

Runes The letters of the Viking alphabet. All the characters are formed of straight lines, which made them easier to carve.

Sacrifice An offering made to the gods to please them. The Vikings offered gifts of jewelry and weapons to the gods and sometimes made human sacrifices.

Sagas A group of prose stories that tell of the exploits of Viking gods and heroes. The sagas were written down in the 13th century.

Seer A person who can supposedly see into the future.

Skald A professional Viking poet.

Soapstone A soft stone found in Scandinavia, which was often used for Viking carvings.

Stern The rear of a ship.

Thing The name of the local councils that ruled Viking communities.

Thrall A slave or landless peasant in Viking society.

Warp The threads that run lengthwise (vertically) in woven material.

Weft The threads that run crosswise (horizontally) in woven material.

INDEX